D1482433

Living the Questions

Robert A. Raines

WORD BOOKS, PUBLISHER
Waco, Texas

LIVING THE QUESTIONS

ISBN 0-87680-437-7
Library of Congress catalog card number: 76-19530
Printed in the United States of America

Living the Questions

OTHER BOOKS BY ROBERT A. RAINES

Success Is a Moving Target
To Kiss the Joy
Lord, Could You Make It a Little Better?
New Life in the Church
Reshaping the Christian Life
Creative Brooding
The Secular Congregation
Soundings

Dedicated
to
D. F. K.

I want to thank my wife Cindy both for her contribution to the design of this book and for her unflinching critique of its various drafts. Her work has added substantially to whatever may be its value.

I also want to thank my editor Floyd Thatcher, whose encouragement supplied energy to put the book together, and Dennis Hill, the book's artist, whose patience and skill have added grace to the book.

CONTENTS

LIVING THE QUESTIONS

Be patient toward all that is unsolved in your heart.
And try to love the questions themselves. Do not
seek the answers that cannot be given you because
you would not be able to live them. And the point is
to live everything. Live the questions now. Perhaps
you will then gradually, without noticing it, live
along some distant day into the answer.

Rainer Maria Rilke

Living the questions of life may be a more realistic and
faithful style of Christian living than seeking answers to
those questions. All of us are somewhat suspicious of
"answers" given to us from any external authority,
including the Church and the clergy. We are certainly in a
time when many traditional "answers" are in question.
Questions are more specific and vital connections with
reality than answers could possibly be.

While we all long for the certainty and security that come with absolute and pat answers, and while we all want to feel that God is in our corner, the reality is that we live by faith and not by certainty or security or even knowledge. Faith implies questioning, searching, wondering and hoping. Faith understands life as a journey that never ends.

Such a quest is not a matter of just having questions, but living the questions we have, and even loving the questions. Somehow, we want to live with our fears and hopes and wonderings in the confidence that, trusting the process in this fashion, we shall live our way into the purpose of God and our own fulfillment.

The Bible is a book of journeys and questions—of people asking God questions, and God questioning his people.

This book is comprised of my pressing questions of recent years. I have gone through divorce and remarriage, change of job and geographic location, changing relationship with parents and children, and the breaking and remaking of my self-image and my image of God. My questions come out of the particular pain and promise of this period of my life. Perhaps some of them will be useful to you in naming and living your own questions.

I invite you to join me in a sharing of journeys and questions, day by day, or now and then, or all night long, as you choose.

THE NEXT TWENTY YEARS

The tallest redwood trees in the
world stand in the Muir Woods
State Park in northern California.
Their huge trunks stretch the
length of a football field into
the sky. That range of mountains
and forest took its present shape
and position twelve million
years ago.

As my birthday approaches
I have been pondering
the next twenty years
of my life.

Standing before that tree
on that coastal range
I felt the immensity of time.
Twelve million years from now
who will know or care
what I do with my next
twenty years?

*What does my life mean now
in the context of such a future?*

*By what values, memories and hopes
shall I weigh my options
make my choices
invest my energies
live my life?
For whom and for what?
Where does the ongoing purpose of God
connect with my own meaning?*

14

I NEVER NOTICED THE BIRDS

I first became acquainted with Barbara Fried through her book *The Middle Age Crisis.* Recently in conversation she said, "Adolescence prepares us to live; middle age prepares us to die." Then, noting the delights and discoveries of her own midlife time, and reflecting on her first forty years, she said, "I never noticed the birds."

Two insights stir in me. One is that death is the frame for the picture of the second half of life. We know that in our heads; but it is something else to feel it in our bones and read it between the lines in our faces. Such awareness is threatening. It forces us to acknowledge our limits, to accept the dénouement of our dreams, and to taste loss in our mouths. But such awareness is also promising. The sense of transience opens "the eyes of our eyes and the ears of our ears." A leafless mountainside, an ache in the heart, a familiar melody, a tender touch or gentle glance—these birds on the wing dart into our consciousness, waking us to a painful joy: "Eternity in an hour." Loss of our sense of omnipotence may bring the modest gain of readiness to trust in the Lord, and to pray with Mary, "Let it be to me according to your word" (Luke 1:38). The second half of life is potentially a Nicodemus time, when we may be born anew in some cradle of becoming.

The second insight has to do with noticing the birds. I never noticed the birds for the first forty years or so of my life either. I was too busy trying to make it, fulfilling big production quotas for the Lord, the Church, and maybe chiefly for myself. There was little time for walking beside still waters, lifting up my eyes to the hills, or noticing the birds. I neglected the natural. I lost the sense of my creatureliness, and so forfeited nature's healing of mind and body. How sweet it is to notice the birds! I feel a freshening of quietness and confidence, a gracious restoration of strength. And I am beginning to accept, a little, my dying and my living as a loved creature. I am grateful to the anthropologist Loren Eiseley and the poet Theodore Roethke, who have been contemporary psalmists of creation to me in these years. Their writings have nourished my natural roots. And I now appreciate the more than twenty varieties of birds that crowd our feeders and delight our days.

How about you?
Been noticing any birds lately?

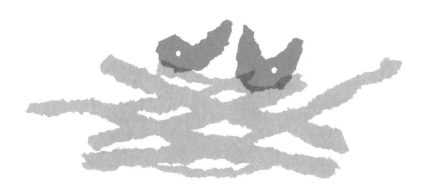

I OFFER MYSELF

Lord,
I offer my needs to you
all that affects my health
I offer my wants to you
all the range of my reaching
I offer my oughts to you
all the duties that define my life
I offer my loves to you
all the people for whom I care

Help me to understand what I need
for my own survival
and what I can get along without
Help me to find a healthy balance
between my wants and my oughts
and give me the wisdom to know
you are in both
Heal and hallow all my loves
that my caring may be
clear and honest

Help me discern when I should
deny myself
for the sake of others
and when I must
affirm myself
for my own sake

I long for leading
I wish the decision
would make itself
I can't meet everybody's
expectations
I can't prevent everyone's hurts

What matters most?
No one can tell me
No one

I have to decide alone

Lord,
I offer myself to you

GOD'S PEOPLE ON THE MOVE

"Come Back, Little Sheba" was a film several years ago, the title of which has stuck with me. It expresses my hope for us as we roll into the fall, and the beginning again of our life and work together.

Come back, little Sheba, Sally, Mary. Come back, big John, Jim, Bill.
Come back from all the vacations and rest and glorious diversions of summer.
Come back from drifting, dozing, and
preoccupation with private pleasure.

Come back to go ahead,
to go ahead together as God's people on the move.
To go ahead in exploring direction and meaning
for our lives as individuals and together.
To go ahead in shaping the uses of our common
energy, dreams, and resources.
To go ahead in offering ourselves to be used by God
in his healing work in our families,
on our jobs, in our city and nation.

Come back to begin again.
To begin again the search for integrity and meaning.
To begin again the work of sharing the suffering
of people—the least of these around us,
and the most of these too.
To begin again the digging together for insight and
strength in our faith and fellowship.

Come back to worship.
There is no substitute for being together, face to face,
singing, crying, dancing, praying, waiting, hoping, loving.
Worship is nothing less than the Spirit of God
in our midst, wakening, opening, disturbing, delighting us.

Come back to sing a new song,
leap over a barrier,
break through a problem,
unlock a purpose,
restore hope,
renew faith,
rekindle love,
and participate in the life of
God's people on the move.

STRETCH OUR SYMPATHIES

Lord, we yearn towards people
   whose faces are strange to us
         faces crying over coffins
         faces staring out of barred windows
     child faces innocent in danger
     aged faces pleated with patience

Deliver us from pride of achievement
to reach out
to those whose need
beckons

Deliver us from self-preoccupation
to occupy ourselves
with neighbors
far
and
near

Kindle our kindness
Bend our reluctance

Draw us beyond the small circle of
"my kind"
to the large circle of
mankind

Stretch our sympathies
and our dollars
to the measure of
human need

STRETCH OUR ENERGIES

Lord, we yearn for our country

   so rich in good will
   so torn with greed and fear

   so blessed with resources
   so in love with power

   so innocent
   so corrupt

Give us eyes and spirit to discern

   truth from propaganda
   integrity from image
   compassion from rhetoric
   wisdom from information

Help us to

   take responsibility for our power
   admit our mistakes
   forgive one another

            and

Stretch our energies

   towards our own healing
   and the healing of humanity

WHEN THE SUNLIGHT COMES

The ice stretched across the river
almost to the west bank
where a few yards of water were flowing free.
It made me think of my own life:
much of it frozen over, covered, stable, dependable,
yet movement and flux nearby.
How the currents swirl under the ice.
A little sunlight can melt it all in a few hours,
to flow free, fast, and newly alive.

I think of my friend at lunch,
listening to his story,
discovering how much is going on under the ice.
I felt kinship with him,
struggling, stretching.
How will it be with him when the sunlight comes,
the ice breaks up,
and things flow free, fast, and newly alive?

Just when I think I have it all together
it begins to come apart somewhere;
and just when everything seems to be falling to pieces
there is a quiet place and a knitting.
I want so much not to miss the beauty, the love,
the meaning of it all.
I yearn for a kind of communication
with those I love
that is unarmored,
without special motive,
clear and caring.
How will it be with me when the sunlight comes,
the ice breaks up,
and things flow free, fast, and newly alive?

DRAGONS AND PRINCESSES

One night several years ago, I was sitting at a table with members of my T-group in Bethel, Maine. In the sparring conversation a sore spot was touched in me. An ache started moving. I knew I was going to cry. I hadn't cried for years, maybe decades. I resisted; my neck muscles distended until my chin hit the table and the tears of forty years poured out. The heaving hurts of all my life shook loose the tight identities of person and profession. The frail structures of my inner and outer being were overwhelmed. I went out into the night alone, groping among my multiple selves.

*And Jacob was left alone; and a man wrestled
with him until the breaking of the day.*

Do you know what it is to be mugged by some awful power in the night? Sometimes an inner ache breaks the bonds of polite control and leaves us quivering with questions. Sometimes external events destroy our neat/obsolete design in the sky and leave us shivering with fearful fantasies.

*When the man saw that he did not prevail
against Jacob, he touched the hollow of his
thigh and Jacob's thigh was put out of joint as
he wrestled with him. Then he said, "Let me go,
for the day is breaking." But Jacob said, "I will
not let you go, unless you bless me." And he
said to him, "What is your name?" And he said,
"Jacob." Then he said, "Your name shall no
more be called Jacob, but Israel, for you have
striven with God and with men and have
prevailed.".... And there he blessed him.*

As a child I learned to deny my demons in the dark, repress my negative feelings, hold in my tears, muffle my passion, and cover my anger. Surface harmony at the cost of emotional honesty. Premature turning of the other cheek. Letting the demon go without a blessing. Since Bethel, I have been learning that the way to drain my demons of their destructivity is to wrestle them to a blessing, to refuse to let them go until they yield me their creative energy.

The demon in the dark is the voice of generative energy within us speaking through dreams or conscious meditation, breaking through our anger and ecstasy, pouring out in every tear. When we have courage to identify with that which haunts us, to embrace the inner stranger, we are transformed. When I can admit my fears to another person who honors them and holds them for me to see, they become even friendly, like Maurice Sendak's Wild Things or Max Ernst's Dark Forests.

Sometimes my demons turn into angels before my eyes. The poet Rilke asks, "How should we be able to forget those ancient myths that are at the beginning of all peoples, the myths about dragons that at the last moment turn into princesses; perhaps the dragons of our lives are princesses who are only waiting to see us once beautiful and brave." Our dragons . . . princesses? Our demons . . . angels? Our assailant . . . God?

> *So Jacob called the name of the place Peniel,*
> *saying, "For I have seen God face to face, and*
> *yet my life is preserved." The sun rose upon*
> *him as he passed . . . limping.*

Jacob was named and lamed. You and I will be
given a new name, a new identity, if we struggle to the
dawn-death, and a scar to remember it by. No naming
without a laming. God scars those he names with some
mark of meaning, some thorn in the flesh which we bear
in our bodies all our days to remind us we have seen
God face to face.

What is your name?
Where are you lame?
Are you limping in the daylight?

Scripture: Genesis 32:24-31, RSV.

THE SECRET PLACES

I CALL TO YOU
FROM THE secret PLACES
OF MY SOUL

    HEAR MY ACHE
    TOUCH MY FEAR
    SEE MY SORROW
    TASTE MY REMORSE

YOU CALL TO ME
FROM THE secret PLACES
OF MY SOUL

    HEAR MY HEALING
    TOUCH MY COMFORT
    SEE MY WISDOM
    TASTE MY PARDON

DEEP CALLS TO DEEP
IN THE secret PLACES
OF MY SOUL

IF I AM MAKING A MISTAKE

O God
if I am making a mistake
let me know
before it's too late

I'm afraid

sometimes
I wish that circumstances
or other people
or Somebody
would settle things for me
one way or the other

sometimes
I wish you would open or shut
a door
but I know I will still
have to choose
between doors
and
the best parts of me
don't want to give up that freedom

I want happiness for all those I care about
and my own happiness
Is there any way
happiness can happen
for all?

is my fear only natural
as I reach the final turning
begin to taste my losses
and know in my insides
that things will never be the same again?

or is my fear a red light from you?

or
both?

only in you
can I find peace without
threat
only with you
can I dare to choose
and make myself
so vulnerable

I
am
safe
with
you

THE LEFT HAND OF GOD

In his book *The Way of All the Earth,* John Dunne recalls one of Rilke's stories entitled "The Stranger." Rilke tells how he once received a stranger who was "without rank, without office, without temporal honor, almost without a name." Having some suspicion as to who the stranger was, he asked him, "Do you still remember God?" Reflecting for a time, the stranger answered, "Yes." Then, to reveal his suspicions without directly stating them, Rilke told the stranger a story about God's hands.

He told how God had never really finished man. He told how he determined to send his right hand into the world to take human form, and that he was not fully satisfied with what he learned from this one hand. "I often think," Rilke concluded, "perhaps God's hand is on its way again."

Dunne believes it was Rilke's suspicion that the stranger who asked his hospitality was the left hand of God. He raises the question: If God held all truth in his right hand, and the lifelong pursuit of truth in his left hand—would you choose the right or the left hand of God? It poses a profound question for Christians.

We are those who believe that Jesus was the right hand of God, alive in human history. In some fashion, for us, Jesus is the truth. But it was Jesus himself who said that he would release at his death the spirit of all truth. And, in fact, it is our own experience that we receive truth from many sources in addition to the truth we see in Jesus. Indeed, sometimes the truth received from "strange" persons or sources illuminates, enriches, and may even alter our experience of the truth we see in Jesus.

Surely all truth is of God, reveals God, and leads us to God. From time to time throughout history, people such as Socrates, Thoreau, Martin Luther King remind us that truth is deeper than what may be defined as right and wrong, legal or illegal in a particular time and place.

Truth is alive and personal, and can never be frozen into a code or doctrine. It can never be held or fixed—only LIVED. Truth is the ground of being from which facts spring and then die as new facts spring forth. Truth includes error, incorporates sin, and overcomes evil through suffering love. Whenever we suffer in love, we are in touch with truth.

How do we become "finished" human beings? Perhaps it is by holding with one hand onto the right hand of God, while with the other we constantly reach out for the left hand of God, in a lifelong pursuit of truth.

I LOVE THE MYSTERY

standing on the deck late at night
looking into the glittering dark
my friend said
    "I love the mystery
     I don't have to know
     who or what it is"

yes
I too love the mystery
and profess to know
who and what it is
    "the God of Abraham, Isaac and Jacob
     the father of our Lord Jesus Christ"

yet
I am uneasy
with quick, definite name tags
for the Nameless One

there is a Christian closure
with God
which sometimes is
too certain
    smug
    familiar
    finished
for me

today
I feel more akin to
Abraham and Jacob
than to
Peter and Paul

more a pilgrim
than a disciple
more a seeker
than a finder
more a learner
than a teacher

"Lo, I tell you a mystery"

but the mystery is larger
than the telling
it eludes our boundaries
it escapes our
    taming
    and
    naming

I love the mystery

WHO HIDES IN YOU?

René Dubos, a renowned French scientist, tapped my curiosity in his book *A God Within.* He reminds us that "the preclassical Greeks symbolized the hidden aspects of man's nature, in particular the forces that motivate him to perform memorable deeds, by the word *entheos*— a god within. From *entheos* is derived the word 'enthusiasm.' . . ."

Dubos suggests that enthusiasm is the source of creativity, the poet's muse, the divine madness which, according to Plato, is "in reality the greatest of blessings . . . which comes from God, is superior to sanity, which is of human origin." Dubos goes on to point out that the words "genius" and "spirit," when used to denote the distinctive characteristics of a given region, city, or institution, imply "the tacit acknowledgment that each place possesses a set of attributes that determines the uniqueness of its landscape and its people."

I was struck by the thought that each person, each institution—whether church, university, city, or nation—has a "genius," a unique endowment of individuality which waits to be born and to come to full bloom. Our task as parents, politicians, and leaders of institutions is to be artists who uncover and release the "genius" or "spirit" of a person or institution, rather than imposing our own molds upon them. As Michelangelo wrote:

> The best of artists has that thought alone
> Which is contained within the marble shell;
> The sculptor's hand can only break the spell
> To free the figures slumbering in the stone.

As a child has certain potentialities to enable him to become a musician, or an athlete, or a leader of people, so an institution is endowed with a special "genius" which derives from the givens of its heritage, history, place, and time.

Dubos writes that "students of Eskimo culture have found that these people . . . attempt to recognize the spirit they assume to be present in natural objects and . . . then to help the spirit to emerge into the open. . . . As the carver held the raw fragment of ivory in his hand, he turned it gently this way and that way, whispering to it, 'Who are you? Who hides in you?' "

One may look at his child, friend, spouse, colleague, and say, "Who are you? Who hides in you?", seeking gently and firmly to enable the release of the unique spirit inside the other. One who cares about a particular institution may similarly deal with it patiently and firmly, seeking the release of its human and other potentials. One may even hold himself gently in his arms and allow his own unique spirit room in which to be born.

There is a unique "spirit," a "genius," a god within each of us and each of our institutions, waiting to be born afresh. Our task is to let it be, indeed to help it be—gently, patiently, firmly, hopefully.

WHY HAVE YOU LEFT ME ALONE?

I feel like a motherless child
I can't go home again
it's too late
I'm too old
my parents can't understand me
nor my spouse, children, friends

I share a part of myself
with this person
another part with that person
but my whole self
with no one

my individuality
clarifies and sharpens
but is itself
a bar
a fence
a wall

am I unwilling to be known
or afraid
or just don't know how?

Augustine prayed:
"our hearts are restless
til they find their rest in Thee."

will I always be alone
in this life?

Jesus was lonely
"foxes have holes, birds of the air have nests,
but I have no place to lay my head."

Jesus was alone
"my God, my God, why have you left me alone?"

there is no answer to that question
this side of death
for Jesus
or me
or anyone

Lord
help me live my loneliness
by accepting it
let your comfort come to me
and your assurance steal over me
that my heart may come to rest
in you
for a moment
or a little longer

DON'T PLAY HOOKY

my friend said to me:

God is working in the loosening of your life
        emptying you of certainties
        breaking your self-image
            as a man who could never choose this
            or would always do that
        making you suffer the loneliness
            of having escaped your own skin
        crowding you with the presence
            of an inner stranger
for you do not yet know yourself

Don't play hooky from God now
    don't pray just for others
    pray for yourself
that you may be able to trust God
    working in the dark of you
that you may be willing to
    experience the pain of his presence
not evading or avoiding
what matters now is not whether
    you were disobedient
    or obedient
    or confused
what matters now is that
    the old images are breaking
    your images of yourself
                other selves
                the will of God

God is kneading you like clay
molding your stubborn will
to be supple in his spirit
let him shape you

there is coming to you
the grace of a new
self-understanding
pehaps even
the peace of a new
self-acceptance

you will be learning
who you are
all by
yourself

WHO AM I
WHEN I AM NOT WORKING?

A lack of energy loosens me this morning
I am waiting for my life to catch up with me
A fallow time

The injunction to get busy and produce
still pokes me
but I am smiling at it today

Being out of harness
and losing my grip on routine
threatens
but also
intrigues me

Who am I when I am not working?
I don't know
but it's time I found out

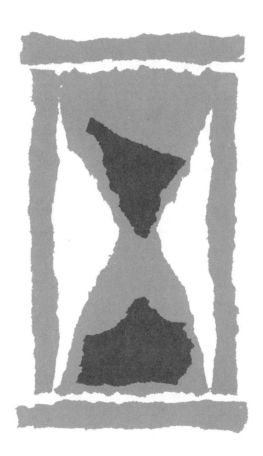

THE TIME OF SELF-KNOWLEDGE

I have a friend by the name of Murtha
who had a plaque on his door
which read
"Murtha Here"

Henri Nouwen wrote:
"to be at home in your own house
means to discover the center of your life
in your own heart"

One day I sat in my study
and let a few words
taste
resonate
penetrate
> *let me live in peace*
> *at home with You*
> *all the days of my life*

I let those words sink down
and dwell in my private space
bringing quietness
and confidence
for a time

Heschel wrote:
"the words of the liturgy
are footholds for the soul"

Sometimes
words of Scripture, hymn, or prayer
are footholds for my soul
becoming flesh in me
leavening my inner space

I need such times of concentration
when the particles of the self
move into alignment
when I can be at home
with myself

Raines here

WHAT'S HAPPENIN', MAN?

My daughter grins and drawls
"what's happenin', man?"

a friend of mine
needs to be
on the cutting edge
with the avant garde
where it's *happening*
and
he needs to have me know
he's there

that's all right
I understand
we fear that history is *happening* to
someone else
somewhere else
        that we are not
where the action is

but history is not to be identified
only as current events
or visible developments
Thoreau was also interested
in another kind of history
inner history
hidden *happenings*

I have a new respect for living
which is not only
on the cutting edge
but also
from the inside out

another friend
once told me that
there are some advantages
in being behind the times

what's *happening?*

God
is
behind me
before me
beyond me
within me

now

ONCE MORE

Lord of little things
    you made your home
    in a stable under a star
    in a cradle on straw
and the little things
shone their starlit welcome
    make your home with me
    in the little things of my days
    cards, gifts, mistletoe on tiptoe
    tree tinsel, multicolored lights
and let the little things
shine their glory for you and me
once more

Lord of little creatures
    you made your home
    in a shelter for animals
    attended by donkey and ox,
    also sheep on a near hillside
and the little creatures
sounded their earthy welcome
    make your home with me
    and the little creatures of my days
    now that the ducks have gone
    and the wild geese,
    waken me to my wildness
    my rabbit-running, deer-leaping heart
    comfort me with the affectionate pawing
    of my dog, or the purring of my cat
    delight me with the bird-flutter
    at my feeder, and
    the wings swooping low over rooftops

and let the little creatures
sound their earthy angel-song for you and me
once more

Lord of little people
    you made your home
    with peasant parents
    nameless shepherds, gifted searchers
and the little people
reached out to touch you
    in wondering welcome
make your home with me
    and the little people of my days
    star-eyed children peeking, hiding
    grown-up children loving, lonely
    white-haired children, remembering, yearning
sit with me in the empty chair at the table
meet me in the postman at the door
stand beside me in the friendship of the years
and let the little people reach their arms
    around you and me
once more

Lord of little me
    you made your home
    in the heart of my world
    make your home now
    in the world of my heart
Love me lonely
only loving you.

Welcome little Lord
Lord of little me
Once more.

THE LAST TIME I SAW MARY

The last time I saw Mary was in November, 1974.
She was excited about her work in the city,
pleased with the development of her two sons,
alive to her life's meaning.
Widowed now seventeen years, she knew who she was.
There was a sparkle in her eyes,
a quiet dignity in her face.
She was a lady.
The cancer was already big in her.
Two months later Mary was dead.

The first time I saw Mary was in 1957.
A mutual friend brought her in to talk
about being the church secretary. Freshly
widowed then, she was demure and uncertain,
like a frightened deer. She took the job.

We watched Mary, over the years that followed,
blossom into a civil rights leader,
a one-woman support system
to people working for social justice
all across the city.

She belonged to so many people.
While she maintained the fundamental loyalties
of family and friends, she lived loyalties
larger and more inclusive.
Though she traveled little,
she became a citizen of the world in mind and spirit.

What a friend we had in Mary!
Understanding that could take us as we really were.
Months, years might go by without much communication,
but when we needed her again
she was there, ready to take up where we had left off.
She would help us move our belongings to another city.
She helped us pick up the pieces of our lives.
She was there for us, always there.

She wasn't one of the best stenographers I've known,
just one of the best human beings.
She was one of those rare persons
who have passionate convictions, yet without
self-righteousness or self-importance
or a need to work off hostility on others.
She had her own sorrows, but was not bitter.
Her pain weathered into a warm understanding
that never lost its wink.

She loved us with a love
that envied not,
was not conceited,
did not insist on its own way.
She bore, believed, hoped, and endured
all things for us and with us.
I felt loved like that by Mary,
loved more than I deserved,
loved more than I returned.
I have lost one of the half dozen
people in this world, outside my family,
whose love I knew I could count on
absolutely.

Mary was a Christian.
She trusted God
with her eyes open to evil
and alert to tragedy.
She had a joy that endured.
She was an Easter person in this world,
a salt-of-the-earth saint.

Good-by, Mary.
See you.

MARY

GOING OUT NOT KNOWING

In recent years as I struggled to find my way, my image of God's will broke. I had thought of God's will as something objective out there in the Bible or in some authority—ecclesiastical, civil, societal, parental. Something I was supposed to decipher and do. Some totting up of the pros and cons of things that would produce The Answer. But in my searching I could find no balance sheet to yield The Answer, no counselor to make my decisions for me, no certified rule of right, no prayer to make things clear, no blessed assurance. I had to make my own decisions in the dark, own them, pay the costs for them, and take responsibility for my own life.

It was like that for Abraham. He had to decide whether to stay in his homeland or follow a haunting promise. He didn't have The Answer any more than we do. We can just hear his relatives and friends saying, "Abe, you 75-year-old idiot! Forget that crazy trip. You've got it made right here. Enjoy, Abe, enjoy!"

But Abraham and his family moved out and shoved off, destination unknown. The terse verse in Hebrews (11:8, RSV) reads: "By faith Abraham obeyed when he was called to go out to a place which he was to receive as an inheritance; and he went out, not knowing where he was to go."
Going out not knowing. Four words that define faith.

I don't think Abraham had some ethereal "religious" experience. I believe that human needs and wants, bread-and-butter fears and hopes, were the raw material of his choices as of ours. God is in our guts. God is in those deep primal energies that power our being and doing more fundamentally than our conceptualizations.

People are insecure these days, and frightened of uncertainty. So there is severe pressure on all of us to drain the mystery, identify insiders and outsiders, and arrive at early closure of our questions. Some people are always trying to swing the gates of the theological OK Corral back in place. Too bad. The nostalgia is understandable, but theological rectitude isn't where it's at. People worrying about a job, holding onto their marriage by the fingernails, or struggling to make it alone, or searching in broken images for the reality of God in their lives aren't into protecting orthodoxy. They're into trying to make it on faith, and in faith. They want to discover what it means to go out not knowing.

And the poets are more help than the theologians. Theodore Roethke wrote, "I learn by going where I have to go." Going is knowing. Wallace Stevens cautions us:

Throw away the lights, the definitions,
and say of what you see in the dark
that it is this or that it is that,
but do not use rotted names . . .
nothing must stand between you and the shapes you take
when the crust of shape has been destroyed.

Rotted names are the names of what other people or we ourselves think we *should* think, feel, be or do. Real names are the names of what we *do* think and feel, what we *decide* to be and do.

God is with us, as with Abraham, in the dark of our deciding. He preserves our going out and our coming in.

Look into your own dark. Listen to the sound of your own sighing.
Trust your own meaning.

The sign of God is that we will be led where we did not plan to go.

LIMITS

people like me
want and need limits
within which to feel secure
against which to find
our own identity
distance
privacy

people like me
strain to set up our lives
and those of others
with prescriptions
so that we can manage
if not control them

people like me
have to exceed limits
to define our inner direction
to become strong enough
in our own eyes
to use limits
as clues
and no longer
as bonds
we need to develop "do's"
so compelling
we can survive the "don't's"

people like me
make agendas
for ourselves and others
uneasy with ambiguity
we seek certainty
insecure with open-endedness
we seek early closure
we are afraid
to trust and to believe

> Lord
> make me graceful
> within limits
> and
> without limits
> let me be
> at ease with my own direction
> sensitive to that of others
> respectful of customs and procedures
> patient towards my own unfolding
> trusting where I cannot manage
> believing where I cannot see

HOW MUCH FREEDOM
DO YOU FEEL YOU HAVE?

My brother wrote me:
"How much freedom do you feel you have?
  What would you be willing to consider?"

his questions set my imagination
spinning

what are the limits to my freedom?
who sets those limits?
my culture sets them
my loyalties and obligations set them
my needs and wants set them
my strengths and weaknesses set them
my knowledge and ignorance set them
other people's choices set them
luck, chance, fate set them
I set them

would I consider
leaving my job
changing professions
moving to another part of the country
risking my reputation
jeopardizing my financial security?
who will pay me what I need
to do what they want to have done?
Do I want to do it?

there moves in me
a power
calling me beyond a particular
relationship, role, or place
to go where I must go
and be who I must be

How much freedom do you feel you have?
What would you be willing to consider?

MY FRAIL RAFT

I love walking at the river alone
it is quiet there
the river flowing on
ever on
like my life

     You are with me
     beside still waters
     near swift waters
     in the rapids
     in the quiet

Grant me in my frail raft
not to struggle
against the current of your leading
but to yield
to the flow of your pressure

You are with me
beside still waters
near swift waters
in the rapids
in the quiet

Let pressure from within
yield clarity
let pressure from without
distill patience
let me sense in every pressure
your presence

You are with me
beside still waters
near swift waters
in the rapids
in the quiet

I AM HAPPENING

There is in me a process of
renascence

the shadow side emerging
my demons surfacing
to join my angels
discovering my dark power of being
unlocking the inner self

there is a strange momentum
about what is happening
in me

I am in gestation
giving birth to myself
yielding self-knowledge

it is a time for quiet eyes
a time to be simple
                private
                    rooted
a time to follow the meaning
and trust it

I believe
God is in what is happening
in me

I am being freed from the past
with appreciation
and freed for the future
with readiness

a particular hope is shaping
a careful joy is rising

don't hurry it
don't analyze it

it is being given
even as
it is being received

I am happening

LET OUR VISION REACH

O Lord
refresh our hopes for ourselves
and our nation.
We are troubled and bewildered.
We see corruption in high places
and know that we ourselves are not immune
to the temptations of power
or the corrosions of privilege.
We see narrow interests prevail
over larger loyalties,
and we would have our own loyalties
set in order
and our own priorities
brought to focus.

Give those in authority over us
grace to do those things
which will invite confidence in their office
and trust in themselves.
Let not a spirit of vindictiveness
make us vengeful towards
those who do wrong,
but let us pursue justice with mercy
as those who know that we ourselves
are not without sin.

Let our vision reach beyond the next deal,
the next election,
to that truth which alone can set us free,
and that candor which alone can restore our trust.
If we have become wise as serpents
restore also to us the innocence of doves
that we be neither bitter nor cynical
but aware of our frailty
and the frailty of all people,
modest in the assumption of our virtue
generous in affirming the virtue of others.

Lift us beyond our own immediate advantage
that we may come to the aid of
those who are without power to exercise their liberty
and those who are without liberty to exercise their power.
Renew in us a soaring spirit
and restore to us that vision without which we perish
that walking together in justice
we may make peace on earth.
Amen.

THE SWINGING DOOR

While rereading *King Lear* recently, I was struck by
the change in Lear from a bitterly judgmental spirit to a
compassionate and understanding person.

In the beginning, anybody who countered his will or
what he thought was right, Lear identified as hostile and
disloyal. Included among those who felt his wrath were
his own daughter, Cordelia, and his most loyal follower,
Kent. But in the course of the play, he painfully comes to
realize that he has charged them wrongly. His own
suffering opens him to the suffering of others. Finally he
breaks through the condemning spirit and cries out,
"None does offend, none, I say, none."

It is a rare, remarkable insight he is expressing, since all of
us offend in one way or another. Therefore, none of us
can judge another: only God may judge. Since all of us
need forgiveness, all of us are set free to forgive. Jesus'
word from the cross put it unmistakably, "Father, forgive
them, for they know not what they do."

Easter means forgiveness, a new possibility of
reconciliation. It has always moved me that the first
appearance of the risen Christ was to Peter, who had
denied him. It comforts and exalts me to realize that he
may always appear to me, who denies him in one way or
another. I trust that he forgives us not only when we
know not what we do, but even when we know what we
do. Yet we can receive his forgiveness only by giving his
forgiveness to others. An unforgiving attitude toward
persons blocks our capacity to receive God's forgiveness.

Forgiveness is a swinging door. If it gets stuck anywhere in our relationships, it gets stuck to some degree everywhere. Who is it hard for you to forgive today? Who may find it hard to forgive you today? Maybe one reason I am so stuck on forgiveness is that I seem to need so much of it so much of the time. The cross of Christ reminds us by its light that all of us cast shadows. In the knowledge of my own shadow-casting, I can hope for my brother the kind of forgiveness I know I need for myself. Therefore, none does offend, none, I say, none. Easter encourages us to make the small gestures and words which may swing open the doors of forgiveness at home, on the job, in the church, and in the broader community.

Forgiveness is a swinging door.

I LONG TO BE KNOWN BY MY CHILDREN

Sun pouring in the large east windows
I started the coffee
shook seed into the bird feeders
and walked down below the house
into the long cut to the salt block
clear hoofmarks in the mud
deer

I stood alone
satisfied
air cold and quiet on my face

sadness crept in

I looked at my children's picture this morning
I miss them so
the dailiness of living in the same house
the time when we were a happy family together

I long to be known by my children
not just as their father
but as I am in my own self

with my strengths and weaknesses
without pretense or apology
known in my humanness

I find myself relating to them now
no longer as a family group
but one to one
to each as an individual
exchanging letters with each
discovering the ways in which
each relationship is unique
to be understood, shared, and fostered
in particular ways
not fearing the diversity
but enjoying it
the parental role abides
the personal knowing deepens
I long to be known by my children

I stand alone by the salt block
and think of each child
pray for each one
and for myself
not without tears
and smiles

SHELTER

water running down the airplane window
like tears
people walking with umbrellas
for shelter
      shelter
      I need
      shelter
      Lord

      heal the wounds
      of those I have wounded
      and my wounds

      lead me
      walk beside me
      follow me

      let forgiveness
      take my arms
      and hope
      invite my feet

            shelter us all
            toward a time
            of
            safety
            and
            confidence

OUT
OF
THE
SILENCE

on our mountain
this morning
a loud chattering
of birds
in the woods
then
silence

then
out of the silence
hundreds of birds
rising
swooping over treetops
winging southward

consider the birds
of the air . . .

sometimes
out of the silence
the energy of hope
rises in me
lending me
wings
for the future

be
still
and
know

KIND AND SAD

I watched Hugh Hefner
being interviewed on tv
on his fiftieth birthday
the interviewer probed for chinks
in the armor of success
any regrets?
any fears?
Hefner would acknowledge none
"the fifties will be my best decade yet"
maybe
we all hope so

in Ingmar Bergman's play
Scenes from a Marriage
Johann says to Marianne,
 "I think perhaps I've stopped defending
 myself. Someone said I'd grown slack
 and gave in too easily. That I diminished
 myself. It's not true. If anything I think
 I've found my right proportions. And that
 I've accepted my limitations with a certain
 humility. That makes me kind and a bit
 mournful."

I feel kind and sad too
midlife yields its own kindness
we can't get kind
until first we get sad
acknowledge our waning powers
admit our fears and
discover compassion
being born
as we are borne
in the arms of experience

we can't always
make it happen
at work
in bed
by faith
or any other way

who am I
when I can't make it happen?

who am I
when I can't keep it from happening?

A TOUGHER SENSE OF

Am I more concerned with
strategy
than
conviction

with what others think
than what I think?

Does my need for approval
cause me to bend myself out of shape
to please others?

Lord
give me a careful reticence
in my expressions of
love for others
that none may feel
unduly bound by obligation
nor tied to expectation
give me a tougher sense of self
that I may value
truth
as much as love
intellect
as much as emotion
honesty
as much as community

I would value
substance
more than
appearance
strategy
less than
conviction

SO LONELY SOMETIMES

So lonely sometimes
yearning toward each other
so near
so far

We're hurting, Lord
heal us

      Let cheeks be radiant
        again and warm
      Let us hear those belly laughs
      Let the looks and touches of love
        be tender
      Let us be gentle with each other
        and patient with ourselves

Spring us loose from yesterday
to trust tomorrow
knowing that in all we are and do
You are with us to the end
and to the beginning again

Hold
us
close
  and
    set us free
to hold
each other
  and
    to let each other go

LANDMARKS

Lord
we praise you
for the nature landmarks of our lives
    mist-laden hills from which your help comes
    shadowed valleys where we may walk without fear
    sun-blessed plains that stretch far
        with your magnanimity

Lord
we praise you
for the people landmarks of our lives
    opponents who force us to
        toughen our truth
        and
        acknowledge theirs
    friends who know us through and through
        and love us still and all
    loved ones who are there
        wherever there is
        always there

Lord
we praise you
for the spirit landmarks of our lives
    laughs that trigger laughs
    tears that just keep coming
    longing that will not be stilled

AND THIS SHALL BE A SIGN UNTO YOU

My nine-year-old son Bob and I were walking
along a road recently when he asked, "Dad, do you
suppose anywhere in the world there is a sign that says
'trespassing'?" I asked what he meant and he said, "Well,
see that sign over there that says 'no trespassing'? Is there
a sign somewhere that just says 'trespassing'?" I laughed
and we had fun imagining what it would be like some
night to change no-signs to yes-signs, from
"no-trespassing" to "trespassing," "private keep out" to
"public come in," changing from "stop" to "go,"
"parking," "safety," etc.

Nature speaks to us in its special sign language. In the
summertime, leaves hide our view of the Appalachian
Ridge. But now in the fall once again we can see that
massive, furry-topped ridge rolling west to north to east,
like the great arm of God coming round to hold us. "I will
lift up mine eyes unto the hills whence cometh my help."

We human beings speak to each other in our special sign
language. There is that sign outside a counselor's office:
"Savage breasts soothed here." And that sign on a
western road: "Choose your rut carefully. You'll be in it
for 20 miles." Last month in a Tulsa congregation, while
singing "All Hail the Power of Jesus' Name," I noticed
some people in the front pews using sign language and

remembered that there is a deaf ministry in that congregation. Their hands moved in a graceful sweep from shoulder to head as we sang, "Crown Him." I was moved. They were turning the no of their condition into a yes to the Lord. . . . A friend shakes hands with his arm extended, signaling to me, "This far but no further." Another responds to my hello by quipping his way behind a fence which keeps me out, anything to preclude self-revelation or personal vulnerability. Am I ready to change a few of my no-signs into yes-signs?

And This Shall Be a Sign Unto You

God speaks to us in his own special sign language—a baby. Not much. A small December child. A baby is birth, beginnings, potential without guarantee. A baby is helpless but not hopeless. A baby is someone to watch. A baby is the future appearing now. Are there baby-signs from God signaling hope to us watchers on the hillsides?

Sir Bernard Lovell, in an article titled "Whence" in the *New York Times,* writes, "We are what we know about where we came from." Reminding us that when we look out into space we are looking back in time as much as 350 million years, he notes with astonishment that if in the first second after the universe burst into being 10 billion years ago "the force of attraction between protons had been only a few percent stronger, the primeval condensate would have turned into helium. No galaxies, no stars, no life would have emerged. It would have been a universe forever unknowable by living creatures." To some watchers on the hillside, the improbable existence of a blue-green earth and its human experiment is a baby-sign in the cosmic void.

Our rising awareness, due to limited energy and food resources, that the survival unit now is no longer the individual nation but the entire human race plus its environment; and our acknowledgment that as our forefathers and mothers declared their independence, so we can now declare our interdependence—this vision is a baby-sign among the flags, floats, and firecrackers of the Bicentennial.

Is there a baby-sign for you and me as individuals? I can only speak for myself. One day last week I saw a road sign with a deer leaping on it, warning motorists to watch for deer crossing the highway. I see myself in that leaping deer and recall Isaiah 35:8, "The lame shall leap like a deer." Beautiful. Are you a leaping deer or a would-be leaper? Are you ready to change a few no-signs in your life to yes, in the season when God's best Yes comes through to us watchers on the hillside?

IT'S SCARY TO GROW UP AT FORTY-NINE

I am trying to accept the fact
that I am alone
I have a spouse, children, parents, friends
but I am alone
I can't depend upon anyone else
for my survival
I am coming into my own
on my own
alone

As I find my own space
and watch others important to me
finding theirs
I am uneasy
I can't manage their lives any longer
much less control them
They are defining
and claiming
themselves

I am glad
for their taking responsibility
Mine for them
has limits
which make it easier for me
to define
and claim
myself

It's scary to grow up at forty-nine
but I've got to

I WILL NO LONGER ASK PERMISSION

I don't want to live
the next period of my life
to meet the expectations of
everybody else
but
to meet my own deepest needs

I will no longer ask permission
to disengage from duty
to others
long enough
to honor duty
to myself

Lord
help me sift
selfishness
from
self-love
help me honor
needs
over expectations
confirm me
or disconfirm me

I'm not sure what you want of me
and for me
but
I believe you are calling to me
in my wants
as in my oughts
in my needs
as in my obligations

help me connect what I want
with what you want

MY ARMS ARE HUNGRY

Lord
bless my dear children
help me accept the loss of
seeing their faces
hearing their voices
feeling their arms
My arms are hungry for them

Let me not hold back my tears
but let them freely flow
as the release of my sorrow
May your tender mercy
ease the pain of my heart
and heal its wounds

Take my might-have-beens
and place them gently aside
in my life's journey
as way stations
I have left behind
And after grieving
may I look to the new days
in glad hope

Let the meanings gather
let me be deepened
tendered
tempered

Let the judgmental spirit in me
be broken
as I am broken
as the bread is broken
for
me

O LORD, ENABLE ME

it is taking more time
               energy
               heart
than I thought would be necessary to
heal

others are nourishing me
reaching out to me
I need them
maybe it's okay for awhile
to be on the receiving end of
encouragement

      O Lord, enable me
             to accept their kindness
             without apology
             or embarrassment

             enable me
             to accept your mercy
             without presuming
             or defending

enable me
to accept myself
without put-down
or put-on

enable me
to accept any I have hurt
damaged in ways
I cannot repair

enable me
to accept any who have hurt me
or misunderstood me
or judged me
and keep a bitter spirit from me

O Lord, let me not wallow in self-pity
nor simmer with resentment
but pick up whatever is my burden
and carry it

LEAP LIKE A DEER

on the farmhouse road at twilight

a white brush

swooped gracefully up

and out of sight

a white-tail deer

leaping

"the lame shall leap like a deer"

"Hear Him, ye deaf; His praise, ye dumb,
  Your loosened tongues employ;
Ye blind, behold your Savior come;
  And leap, ye lame, for joy."

Lord give me grace lame as I am to leap like a deer

WITH GLADNESS OF HEART

You shall have a song as in the night when a holy feast is kept; and gladness of heart, as when one sets out to the sound of the flute to go to the mountain of the Lord. . . .
                                                                        Isaiah 30:29, RSV

O Lord God, our hearts are glad
as we make pilgrimage this day
to our special place;
Here you have touched our bones, whispered in our
    hearts,
and made the ground under our feet holy;
you have gathered us from out of the peoples
and brought us from the separate journeys of our lives
to make festival here together.
Bless us who have come in the mute yearning of our
    years;
and bless those who are present in mind and spirit.

O Lord of this people and all people,
we remember much;
we remember the vision of those special few
who planned, worked, prayed, and gave of themselves
that this company might flourish;
we remember pilgrim souls restored, wounds healed,
spirits refreshed in this place.
Strangers all, you have made us welcome here.
We remember the laughter of many nights, songs in the
    morning,
tears and bitter disappointment, joy upon joy.

Receive our memories offered before you now
as the fragrance of all we cherish.

O Lord of this place and all places,
we hope much.
We seek the energy of your grace
invigorating our common ministry in the time ahead;
we trust you when the fog closes in,
we exult in you when we can see forever;
As you have led us in the past, so guide us, O Thou Great
    Jehovah,
across the years that stretch to the stars;
bear your people on eagles' wings to the promise of our
    land,
even unto the end of our days.

O Lord of this time and all time,
we celebrate much
as a cloud of witnesses gathered to make festival,
        "For lo, the winter is past,
            the rain is over and gone.
        The flowers appear on the earth,
            the time of singing has come,
        and the voice of the turtledove
            is heard in our land."

Amen and amen.

Scripture: Song of Solomon 2:11-12, RSV.

MAKE ME EVER GREEN

O Lord
Your kindness is new
every morning

I delight in the land
blooming ever green
the warm sun on my forehead
the yellow beauty
after a season of rain

Wipe away my tears

Renew the land of my life
Make me ever green

Warm my spirit

Heal the ache of yesterday
Bear me on wings of promise

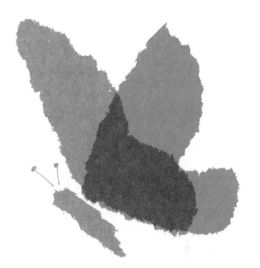

OUR WHOLE BAG

In an informal worship service participants created *luminarios,* or sandbag candles. Each was given a paper bag and marking pencil and asked to make a list of his needs on one side of the bag and a list of his gifts on the other side. The bags were then filled with sand and a candle, lighted, and placed in front of the participant in the congregational circle.

One participant reported that he had a struggle deciding which side of the bag to expose to others and which to face himself. If he exposed his "needs" then he would have to sit there looking at his "gifts." If he exposed his "gifts" then he would have to sit there looking at his "needs." Was it harder to face his gifts with their responsibilities or his needs with their vulnerabilities?

We do well to reach out to one another with our whole bag.

If I share a gift with a friend without letting him know in some way that I also need him, he may feel put down, degraded, and unable or unwilling to accept my gift, acknowledge his need, and understand that he has gifts and I have needs.

If I share a need with a friend without letting him know in some way that I have a gift for him, I may make him fearful that I will depend unduly on him, may encourage in him superiority and avarice, and may thwart his ability to understand that I have gifts and he has needs.

It is as blessed to receive as it is to give.

We are all needy givers and gifted receivers.

We do well to reach out to one another with our whole bag.

THE TRUE EASE
OF YOURSELF

I AM SEEKING A TIME

of personal congruence
when my inside
and outside
will come into
focus
when that which is happening
inside me
will be truly and warmly
reflected in my roles and relationships

WHEN I WILL BE IN PHASE

with my journey

I long for the imperishable quiet
at the heart of form*

ARE YOU SEEKING

a time
of personal congruence?

What springs you loose
    to listen to your insides
    and see your roles and relationships
    real?
What frees you
    to bring your private needs
    and public responsibilities
    in balance?
What releases
    your capacity for intimacy
    while preserving your privacy?

There is a time
    to move again
    in your natural rhythm
a time of seasoning
and quiet ripening

A TIME TO COME UPON
THE TRUE EASE OF YOURSELF*

* the language of Theodore Roethke

THE DAY I LOST POWER

One day I was in charge. The next day I was not.
That day and the days ahead yielded much insight
into roles and relationships.

The man who took care of an essential business service
for me, as a courtesy, while I was Senior Minister,
immediately let me know upon the ending of my role that
the work he did for me from then on would cost me. He
was as good as his word. I should have understood that
his solicitous concern for my business care had more to
do with his need to be related to the Senior Minister than
anything else, more to do with my position than with me.
Insight #1.

A colleague who had been a partner in respect and
affection found his role, with the ending of my role,
changing. A confused mixture of caring and anger,
distrust and support overtook us. Role change disturbed
the relationship.
That can happen.
Insight #2.

Another colleague remained constant in her relationship
to me when my role as her boss ended. Indeed, I found
myself freed from the proprietary feelings one has for
someone who works for him, and she found herself freed

from trying to meet my job expectations of her. A deeper, less complicated relationship developed which gave the mutual affection and respect we shared a way to continue to grow.
Role change facilitated the relationship.
That can happen.
Insight #3.

Some former parishioners sent Christmas cards to me the Christmas after my role as their Senior Minister ended. Many did not. You don't send Christmas cards to a dead role, but to a living person. I realized that many parishioners over the years have related to me, and I to them, primarily in a role, and that when the role ends, there may be little left inside the relationship. Roles are necessary and such relationships can be mutually creative. But one cannot assume non-role loyalties in such relationships, and one can discover only after the role has ended what interpersonal meaning was or wasn't there.
Insight #4.

Insights which emerge in the context of losing power are useful in the context of having power.
Insight #5.

Insight is power.

SAFETY AND VULNERABILITY

There is a time to leave home, and a time to come home:
> a time to hide, and a time to come out of hiding
> a time to advance,and a time to retreat
> a time to make it happen, and a time to let it
> happen
> a time to ask questions, and a time to find
> answers
> a time to be safe, and a time to be vulnerable

Vulnerability exposes us to the ache throbbing in
the heart of the world and in our own hearts. It keeps
us engaged, invested, hurting and therefore hoping.
It keeps us from cold detachment or uncaring cynicism.
Self-mockery provides distance for our aching, a sense
of history and of humor. It protects us against self-pity,
sentimentality, taking ourselves and our causes
too seriously.

To be vulnerable is to suffer loss, to have to learn how to
grieve. To be vulnerable is to have our own judgmental
spirit broken again and again by the acknowledgment of
our own failures and betrayals. It is to lose immunity
against the cries, laughs, and songs of others. When we
become vulnerable, we are accessible to be known.
We receive the gift of self-revelation which is the gift of
intimacy, which is the sharing of privacies. To be human
is to be vulnerable. But to be constantly, totally
vulnerable is to be dehumanized. Survival requires
safety . . . sometimes.

The psalmist writes, "Yahweh Sabaoth, bring us back,/let your face smile on us and we shall be safe" (Ps. 80:3, JB). And again, "Come, let us praise Yahweh joyfully,/acclaiming the Rock of our safety" (Ps. 95:1, JB). Every person has safety needs. Remember that gospel hymn: "Leaning on the everlasting arms . . . safe and secure from all alarms"? Until I grew up and came to know my own need for safety, I associated that hymn with weakness and a need for otherworldly crutches. I know now that there is a time for sanctuary, oasis, shelter. There is a time for licking wounds, restoring the soul, waiting for strength to be renewed. If in Jungian terms the masculine God calls us out of our safety to leave home, the feminine God calls us out of our vulnerability to come home. And blessed are those who have ears to hear their calling.

In Elie Wiesel's drama *The Madness of God,* the interrogator asks the old rabbi, "What is prayer? Is it question or is it answer?" The rabbi replies, "It is both. If you have questions, prayer leads to answers. If you have answers, prayer brings questions." The questioner and answer-giver are one. The rock of our safety lodges in the rapids of our vulnerability. As, one by one, doctrines, visions, strategies, persons, institutions demonstrate their fallibility and mortality . . . wherein does our safety lie?

For me, safety lies in the trust that nothing in life or death can separate me from the love of God come clear in Christ.

There is a time to be safe and a time to be vulnerable. And blessed are those who know the timing of their time.

LORD
LET
ME

Where there is loss
    there is gain.
Where there is sorrow.
    there is wisdom.

There is freedom
    only where there are limits.
There is forgiveness
    only where there are betrayals.

Lord
let
me

Grieve my losses
Ponder my sorrows
Engage my limits
Acknowledge my betrayals

that
I
may

celebrate my gains
weather into wisdom
value my freedom
receive forgiveness

HOMECOMING IS COMING HOME

Homecoming is coming home. Coming home to leaves changing color, to school and college, to football on the tube. Coming home to take up again our routines in the family and the community, at work and in the church.

But we can't go home again. We can't recapture our lost innocence. We can't go back to patterns of feeling and behavior that suited us yesterday. For it is today, and today creates its own urgencies and choices. Nostalgia is real, but it is not reality. We have suffered loss from yesterday even as we bring its gain into today. We can't go home again because people and places change; "The old gray mare ain't what she used to be," and neither are we—for better and for worse.

And yet we can always go home again. Though we may leave home, home never leaves us. Though we stay home, we may never discover what home is until we leave it. Home has to do with our continuities—as persons and as a nation and as creatures on homeland earth. Home is those people and places which nourish our identity and vocation. Home consists of those roots and sources from which the energies of faith, hope, and love pour forth. Home is where the meaning flows, where the heart goes. Home is "something you haven't to deserve." [1] Home is given and forgiven. Home is "wherever the sensibility can defend itself, where humanness can begin to rediscover its outlines against a backdrop of ruins." [2] We can lose home and we can choose home. Home happens where and when we feel at home—in the universe, in our communities of significance, with ourselves. Home has to do with our continuities.

There is a continuity of place. Home, home on the range, in the valley, in the city streets, around the corner, and on the village green. Land where our fathers and mothers lived and died; land where we were married and loved and lived; land where our children were born and grew up and left. There is a significance of place that gives us ground on which to stand, the ground of our being. But this is the day of the mobile home and the bulldozer. Often our significant places are wiped out and we feel a long, long way from home. Where shall we look for the security and comfort of the houses and backyards that are no more? How shall we find or create again a home within the wilderness of our wandering?

There is a continuity of people. There are those significant others with whom we make our home and feel kinship.

Home is where our loved ones are. Home is where the heart abides. Yet people grow up and grow out and grow old. Parents die, children leave, spouses change, friendships are intermittent. And soon or late that aching homesickness comes again to haunt our hopes. And we hold each other against the fear, huddling in the dark, learning that there is no abiding home on this earth.

What shall we do with our homesickness? How shall we honor our homing instinct? In our estrangement and yearning, how can we come home to those significant people and places of our lives? Can we connect again with the roots of our continuities and be restored by their life-giving juices? Can we recreate our country and its values so that once again we can feel at home in it? Can we restore our homeland earth as fit once more for living things? Can we come home to the One who is our eternal home now and forever? Come home! Come home to those special places which for you are holy ground. Come home to those special people who for you make life and love happen. Come home to sing the old, old story with a new, new song. Come home to yourself and to the love of God.

[1] Robert Frost, *Death of The Hired Man*.
[2] Richard Gilman, *New York Times* Book Review, p. 1, June 29, 1975.

... AND WHERE WE CANNOT

grant us grace

    to forgive

        and where we cannot forgive

    to forbear

        and where we cannot forbear

    to understand

        and where we cannot understand

    to accept

FALLING STARS AND LEAVES

last night was cold, clear
stars immediate, diamond-sharp
in the bowl of a sky
      and then
            through the Milky Way
               a falling star

falling stars and leaves

this morning between the boughs
I saw the distant hills along the river
fog hanging low in the valley
a burst of blackbirds just after sunrise
the sun warming my face

where have all the leaves gone?

the time of falling leaves
when the mature colors
present themselves
mauve, russet, amber, plum
their leaves
fading
falling
uncovering boughs bare and real

the shape of the hills abides
the substance that is left
that endures
that holds out for what life means

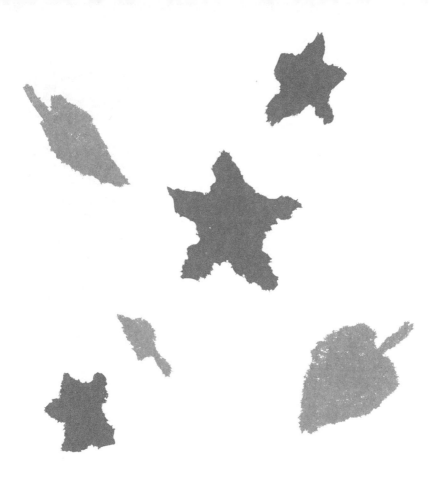

life defines in the autumn
the gathering spirit ripens
in the seasoned flesh of the years
the bones appear
the face weathers
the fruit is borne

there comes a comfortable chill
to the night air
and harvest
draws
near

YESTERDAY'S WILL OF GOD

The Spirit . . . drove him out into the wilderness.
The wilderness image in the Bible is ambivalent,
connoting deprivation, journey, transition, heightened
awareness, chaotic and cleansing silence, aloneness, the
presence of testing. Do you know something of what it is,
with Jesus, to struggle for your identity and vocation in
some wilderness period of your life, a time when a fresh
baptism of the Spirit has blown apart your images of self,
God, life, and left you blinking in the blinding dark?

And he was in the wilderness forty days, tempted by Satan.
Satan begins his questioning of Jesus each of the three
times with the word *if* (Matt. 4:1-11). Jesus was not sure
of something. Should he accept the traditional roles of the
messiah (to be the new prophet, priest, king) prescribed
by his heritage and here articulated by Satan? Satan
hooked into the *ifs* of Jesus.

What are your ifs or agendas from the past, laid on by parents, peers, heritage? How is Satan hooking into your oughts and guilts to predetermine your behavior in conformity with yesterday's will of God?

Satan's function is to make tangible the tension between yesterday's will of God and today's will of God. He makes evil visible and choice unavoidable. He forces the tension between our self and our roles to the tearing point. He smokes us out of our obsolete identities, and tempts us to stay as we are in the roles of the past.

Jesus said *no* each time to Satan's *if,* in order to be free to say *yes* to today's will of God. How are you tempted to accept the roles, agendas, prescriptions of yesterday? What does it mean for you to say *no* to yesterday's will of God, so that today's will of God for you can appear?

While being interviewed about her role in *Alice Doesn't Live Here Anymore*, Ellen Burstyn said, "With other characters I've had to wear a wardrobe. With Alice I could use my own skin. . . . In Strasberg's training, you learn to become strong enough to let your inner life show, which of course includes weaknesses." Satan taunts us to see whether we have courage to live in our own skins where we may be apprehended by today's will of God.

And he was with the wild beasts, and the angels ministered to him.
Beasts and angels gather round every cradle of holy birth, bespeaking the natural and spiritual world, and hinting of the transformation of nature and history, when the lion and lamb shall lie down together, and as Woody Allen sagely notes, the lamb shall get up! A new earth, a new birth.

Cindy saw a clay sculpture on the wall of an art shop. Reddish brown, round, with something white appearing out of a torn, ragged womblike opening—a child's white face. At once frivolous and ominous. Along the top of the sculpture was a number: 45970. Outside a number; inside a name. Who's got your number? Who knows your name?

That clay sculpture, reminding us that we have clay faces and feet, now hangs on the wall of our living room where we are dying to a number and living to a name; dying to a role and living to a self; *no*-ing and *yes*-ing: living in our own skin and loving the skin we're in; dying to yesterday's will of God, and living to today's will of God.

Scripture: Mark 1:12-13, RSV.

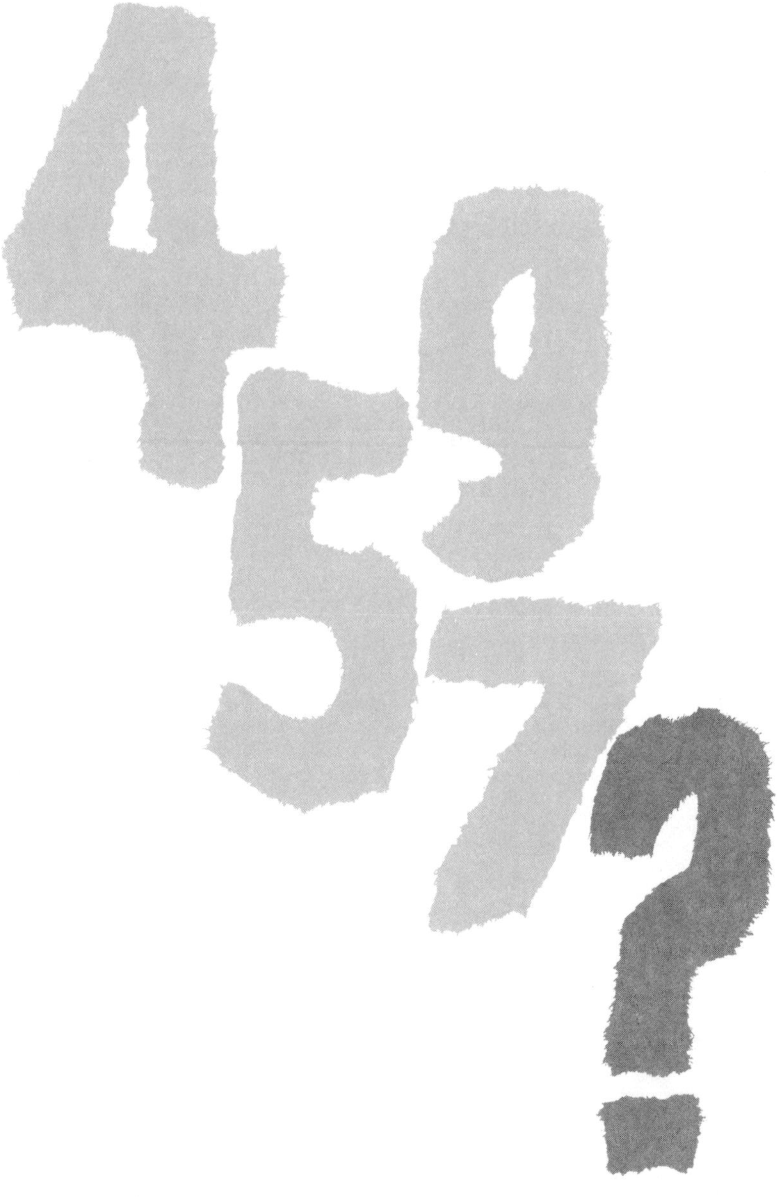
4 5 9 7 ?

I take the leisure
        to consider my days
in the light
        and dark
            of
four billion years